twenty years of inspiration,
intriguing bits and other curiosities

kate spade

NEW YORK

THINGS *we* LOVE

ABRAMS, NEW YORK

Abrams

EDITOR
Deborah Aaronson
Rebecca Kaplan

DESIGN MANAGER
Christine Moog

MANAGING EDITOR
Jen Graham

PRODUCTION MANAGER
Ankur Ghosh

Design:
Rational Beauty
Jeanette Abbink

Photography and Art Consultant:
Kevin Kwan

Library of Congress Cataloging-in-Publication Data

kate spade new york (Firm)
kate spade new york: things we love: twenty years of
inspiration, intriguing bits and other curiosities /
by kate spade new york; introduction by Deborah Lloyd.
pages cm
 ISBN 978-1-4197-0566-3
1. Fashion—Miscellanea. 2. kate spade new york
(Firm)—Miscellanea. I. Title.
 TT507.K348 2013
 746.9'2—dc23
 2012007073

Printed and bound in China
10

Abrams books are available at special discounts when
purchased in quantity for premiums and promotions as
well as fundraising or educational use. Special editions
can also be created to specification. For details, contact
specialsales@abramsbooks.com or the address below.

ABRAMS The Art of Books
115 West 18th Street, New York, NY 10011
abramsbooks.com

contents

foreword

i've long contended that fashion is a party to which everyone is invited. but the woman who expects more from an evening knows that a kate spade new york handbag is her ticket to the vip section.

in 1993, when the eponymous founder and her husband, andy, sent their fleet of accessibly chic black accessories out into the world, the party was officially on. kate and andy have a way of making every day feel glamorous. dinner with the spades is like stepping into an old hollywood blockbuster—only in full color. it's no wonder that by 2007, when kate moved on to other endeavors, the company's *it* status was in the bag.

how fitting, then, that kate's successor turned out to be none other than my fellow brit and longtime cohort deborah lloyd. deborah is an elegant adventurer, equally inclined to wear diamonds for breakfast and to show up at her own wedding in a helicopter (i can attest she's done both, and to great effect). from the moment she arrived at kate spade new york, deborah dove into her new role, bringing her delightful sense of english quirk and whimsy to the all-american brand. i couldn't have written a better sequel.

it helps that deborah basically *is* the kate spade new york woman— timeless yet on trend, dressed for success in every sense of the word. "people tell me that what i wear every day is what most people would wear to a wedding," she joked in a *bazaar* profile.

over the years, it's been a joy to watch the brand grow up, gradually evolving from preppy to polished and expanding beyond handbags into new frontiers in clothing and jewelry. in only twenty years, kate spade new york has become a classic.

and what's more fashionable than that? happy anniversary.

glenda bailey
editor in chief, *harper's bazaar*

introduction

as a child i dreamed of wearing silver dresses and sparkly shoes. in my wildest imagination, i couldn't have conjured a more perfect place to settle someday than kate spade new york. thanks to a lucky twist of fate—and a gentle push from my friend glenda bailey—i was introduced to this brand five years ago and immediately recognized a kindred spirit. i joined as the creative director in 2007, and my amazing journey began.

in my first year i launched jewelry and ready-to-wear, filling both collections with many of the *things we love*: bold colors, statement-making silhouettes and that always unexpected twist—a part of the brand that had charmed me from the start. ideas i'd contemplated for years, but never felt right before, came to life. my obsessive collecting (of cocktail rings, fine china and vintage dresses) suddenly had a grander purpose, sparking new ideas and additions to our *things we love* list.

we've grown quite a bit in the last five years, and it's even more remarkable when you consider where we started twenty years ago. we now have shops from são paulo to shanghai, but we haven't lost sight of who we were when we began. we're still an adventurous, feisty brand with an indomitable spirit and a fearlessness when it comes to standing out from the crowd, staying curious and sharing the things we love most—whether it be a doodle on a cocktail napkin, an off-color quip or our favorite type of champagne (pol roger, if you're wondering). we hope you'll enjoy them as much as we do.

welcome to our colorful world.

deborah lloyd
creative director, kate spade new york

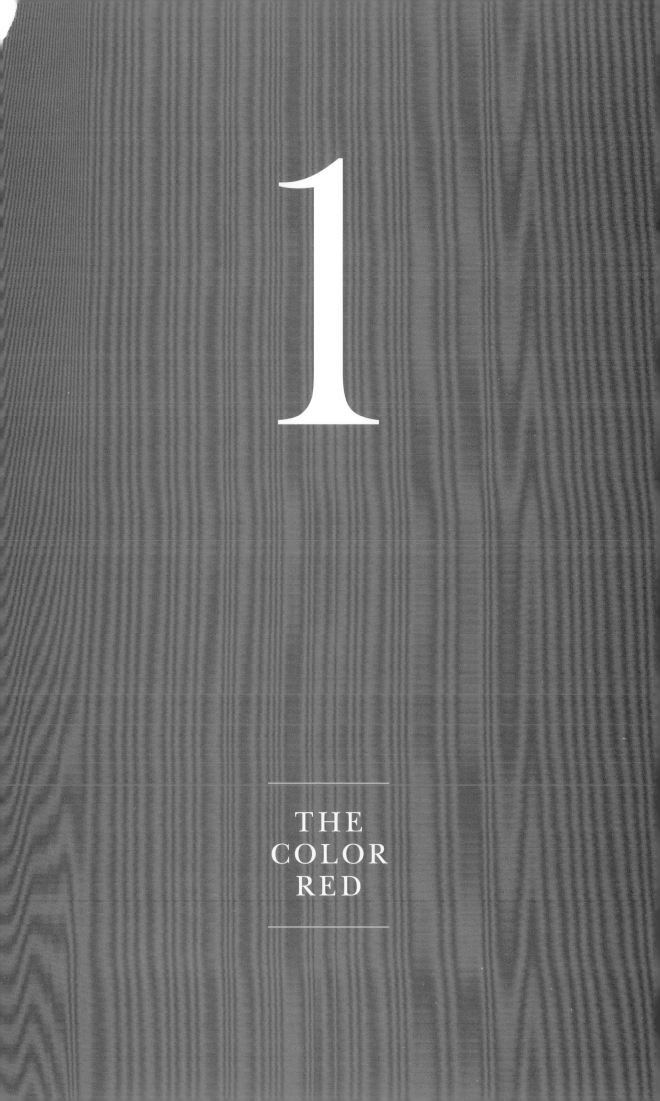

1

THE
COLOR
RED

as a color, red is said to incite a faster heartbeat and induce rapid breathing. it's the reaction we have when we spy, say, the perfect shade of lipstick. it comes in a crayon box of hues, and the shade we choose—time and again—is that perfect orangey red. it's a summer tomato on the vine, handpicked and mashed into a spicy bloody mary. it's a pair of come-hither heels that instantly channels that song by the cure, "hot hot hot!!!" it's powerful in its magnetism, luring even the most color-shy to give it a try with a lunchtime manicure or a chic leather handbag (both make for a colorfully pleasing pop).

B MINE

CONFIDENTIAL

WEAR RED

"i love red so much that
i almost want to paint everything red."
ALEXANDER CALDER

RED LETTER DAY

TAKE HEART

STOP AND SMELL THE ROSES

LONDON C

PAINT THE TOWN RED

ON CALLING

OUR FAVORITE BLOODY MARY*

2 ounces hangar one vodka
4 ounces tomato juice
2 teaspoons worcestershire sauce
2 teaspoons horseradish
¼ teaspoon old bay seasoning
pinch of freshly ground black pepper
½ teaspoon dijon mustard
4 shakes tabasco
1 squeeze each of fresh lemon
   and lime
1 boiled cocktail shrimp
1 cornichon or cocktail pickle

• mix together all ingredients
  except the vodka, cocktail shrimp
  and cornichon.

• rim a highball glass with lemon
  and old bay.

• add 2 ounces vodka over ice and
  fill with the bloody mary mix.

• garnish with a skewered shrimp
  and cornichon.

*courtesy of the mermaid inn, new york, new york

essie "clambake" is our go-to red.

OIL COCKTA

45RPM

S62245A

PENNY SLO

CHAMPA

☺ You will have many adventures.
21 7 26 17 12

REDHEADS 50

CONTENTS
58 SAFETY MATCHES

LO❤E
LO❤E
LO❤E
LO❤E
LO❤E
USA 20c

Nederland
12c
+8

45

SPECIAL DELIVERY

PUCKER UP

valentine

AIR MAIL

PANTONE®
485 C

"a thimbleful of red is redder than a bucketful."
HENRI MATISSE

"WHEN IN DOUBT, WEAR RED."

BILL BLASS

*"give a girl the right shoes
and she can conquer the world."*
MARILYN MONROE

A
WELL-PLACED
BOW

our signature detail, a well-placed bow, is often the finishing touch we turn to when designing a collection. we love this iconic embellishment in all iterations: crafted in lucite for the closure of a handbag, intarsia-knit for a trompe l'oeil twist or smartly starched for a riff on classic menswear (we find a bow tie in particular to be charming on a woman and devastating on a man). traditionally thought of as prim and proper, the bow becomes a bit saucier when we tie it in eye-popping materials and novel textures. to emphasize the placement, we'll play with proportions— a bow is sweet when small and makes a modern statement at a larger scale.

the graphic bow pattern in the image at left was inspired by the signature bows on our handbags.

*"i love the fact that bows can be so
elegant and yet have a sense of humor too."*
DEBORAH LLOYD

"one should always be tempted to untie a woman's clothes." YVES SAINT LAURENT

from one of our favorite
books, *what shall i wear?*
by claire mccardell.

OW TO TAME A SCARF—A SASH—A BOW

It all takes practice, but when you've learned how it's
pure delight. Visualize the figures above without their
identifying scarf or sash or bow. What you would
have is a paper-doll row of identical twins like the ones
you used to cut out of folded paper. Now do you see

why a sure-fire way to add an individual look of Fashion is all wound up in that length of color at your neckline or waistline? There is really only one reason in the world to deny yourself the fun of these Fashion extras: that you *can't* learn to tame them. But you *can*.

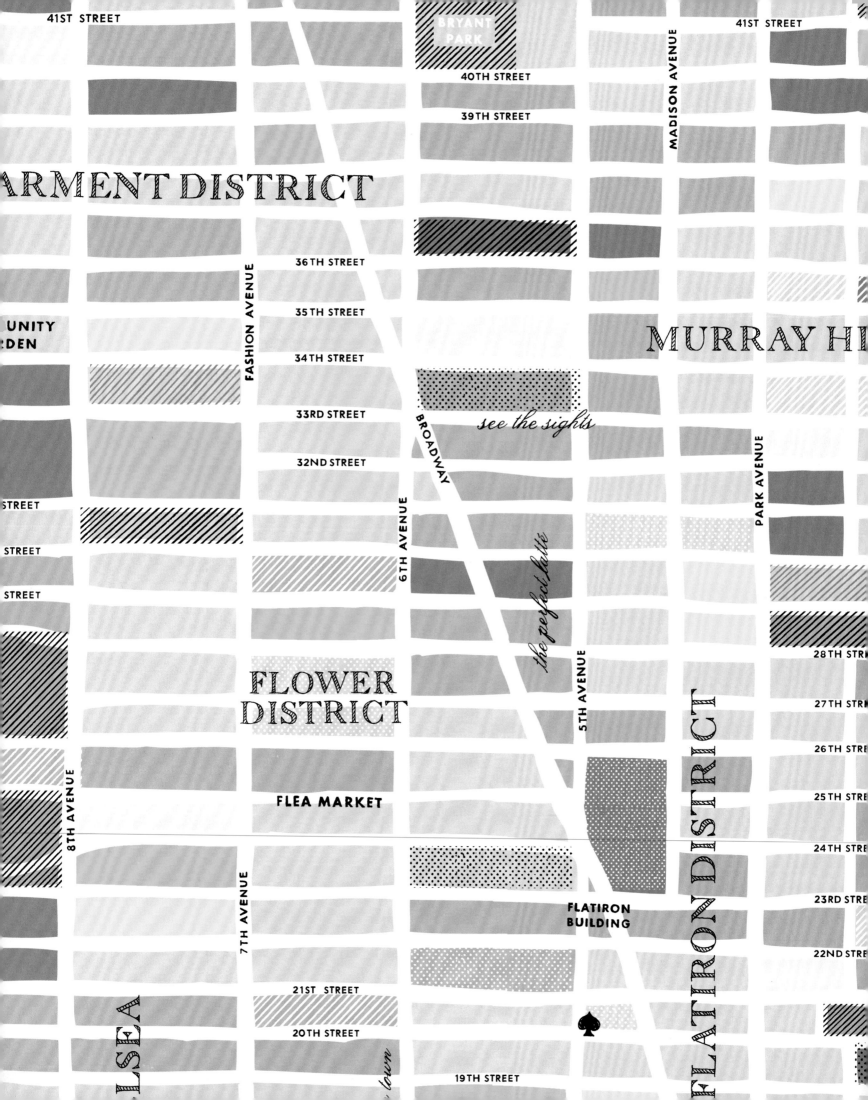

3

NEW
YORK,
NEW
YORK

we ♥ ny. it's in our name, after all. as a brand, we're constantly seeking the sweet spot between the sophisticated highs and the playful lows. we like to think of ourselves as having an uptown sensibility with a downtown edge. so it's only fitting that our favorite place shares our affinity for this great juxtaposition—and as a city, nobody does it better than new york.

take the flower district, near our office. turn the corner on 28th street before 7:00 am on any given weekday and the ordinarily gritty block is transformed by stalls of seasonal flowers, verdant greens and statuesque branches, overflowing and spilling out into the streets. or consider central park. it only takes an afternoon of sunbathing on the great lawn to forget that the grassy respite is located in the heart of the concrete jungle.

for these (and too many more reasons to list) we love new york—a city so nice, they named it twice.

view of the macy's thanksgiving day parade. 1988. the inaugural parade was held in 1924 by employees of the macy's department store, mostly first-generation americans.

NUTS 4 NUTS

UPTOWN

artist andrew coates's
untitled (snowglobe), 2004.

(ecil) BEATON's NEW York.

37th STREET

HIDEAWAY

32 West 37th St.
New York, N.Y.
947-8940-1

DOWNTOWN

HOLIDAY
OCTOBER 1959 · 50¢
NEW YORK

this paper coffee cup became a new
york icon after debuting at city food
carts, delis and diners in the '60s.
more than a billion cups of joe have
been served in them since.

> *"THERE'S SOMETHING IN THE NEW YORK AIR THAT MAKES SLEEP USELESS."*
>
> ——————
>
> **SIMONE DE BEAUVOIR**

as a tribute to nyc, we shot our fall 2009 campaign at some of manhattan's most celebrated haunts. for close to
a quarter century, there was no better place to cap off a late night in the city than restaurant florent (top),
until it closed its doors in 2008. even its matchbooks were memorable, designed by legendary nyc design studio m&co.

the statue of liberty's waistline is thirty-five feet.

oh, new york, why do we love thee? let us count the many ways... 1. outdoor movie nights in bryant park (complete with a fizzy refreshment in plastic glasses and cheddar on triscuits) 2. sipping fresh-squeezed lemonade while strolling the high line 3. browsing the dollar book carts at the strand 4. ice-skating between skyscrapers at rockefeller center and buying roasted chestnuts afterward from the fragrant cart on the corner 5. people watching in paley park 6. food delivery—of any kind—at any time of day! 7. thin-crust pizza at joe's on carmine 8. bicycling along the hudson beside the west side highway (wondering what it is you've spotted in the water) 9. ordering french fries and white sangria at pier i café 10. break-dancers on the subway 11. gallery hopping in chelsea 12. frozen cappuccinos at café angelique 13. "borrowing" a tray from the wollman rink cafeteria and going sledding in the snow 14. lacing up for a spin with the central park roller disco 15. live jazz at smalls 16. leash-free mornings in the park 17. walking across the brooklyn bridge at sunset 18. rooftop barbecues 19. beauty & essex's pawnshop facade 20. sunbathing in sheep meadow 21. cocktails at the campbell apartment 22. late-night pierogi at veselka 23. marveling over the murals at bemelmans 24. the ticket machine at the odeon 25. buying an armload of peonies in the flower district and carrying them home on the M5 downtown 26. indie movie nights at the IFC 27. chatting with the staff at rebel rebel records 28. the halal cart at 53rd and 6th 29. photo booth strips at the ace hotel 30. the little red lighthouse under the george washington bridge 31. dim sum dance parties in chinatown 32. joanne hendricks's cookbooks' shop 33. lying under the great blue whale at the american museum of natural history 34. window-shopping on 5th avenue at christmastime 5TH AVE 35. homemade marshmallows at city bakery 36. playing go fish while waiting for tickets to shakespeare in the park

TAKE THE TRAIN TO THE END OF THE LINE.

for nearly two decades at new york's legendary coney island park,
a stuntman nicknamed "suicide simon" blasted himself out of a cannon twice daily.

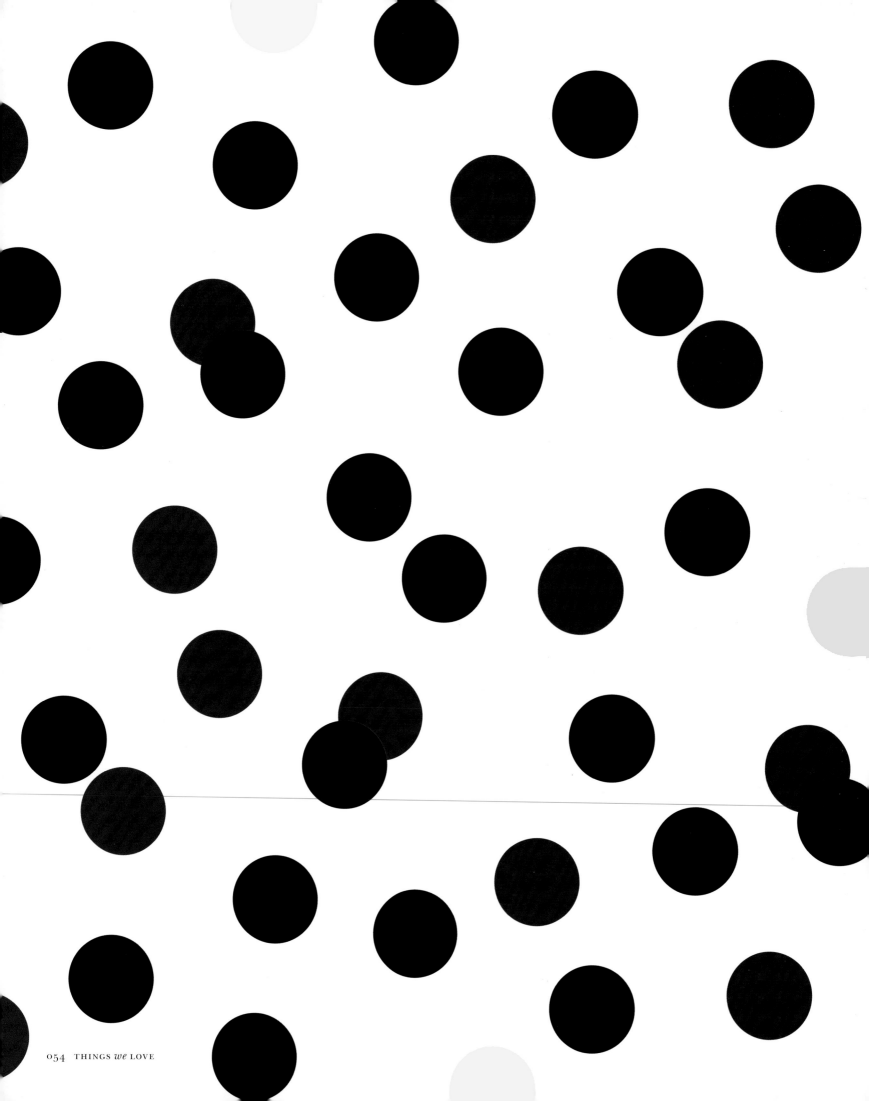

4

THE
POLKA
DOT

one of our longtime favorites, the polka dot is friendly, classic and strong. it's a pattern that we love at all sizes—from delicate swiss dots on a breezy cotton sundress to great graphic dots placed on a chic overcoat.

we love dots in decor, especially in wallpaper and upholstery. we love them sprinkled as confetti or inflated as balloons. we love dots as art—think of the conceptual work of john baldessari or the installations of felice varini.

there's a bold perfection to a dot. it can communicate confidence, like the period at the end of a sentence, though it also makes clear the indecision of an ellipsis and the exuberance of an exclamation point.

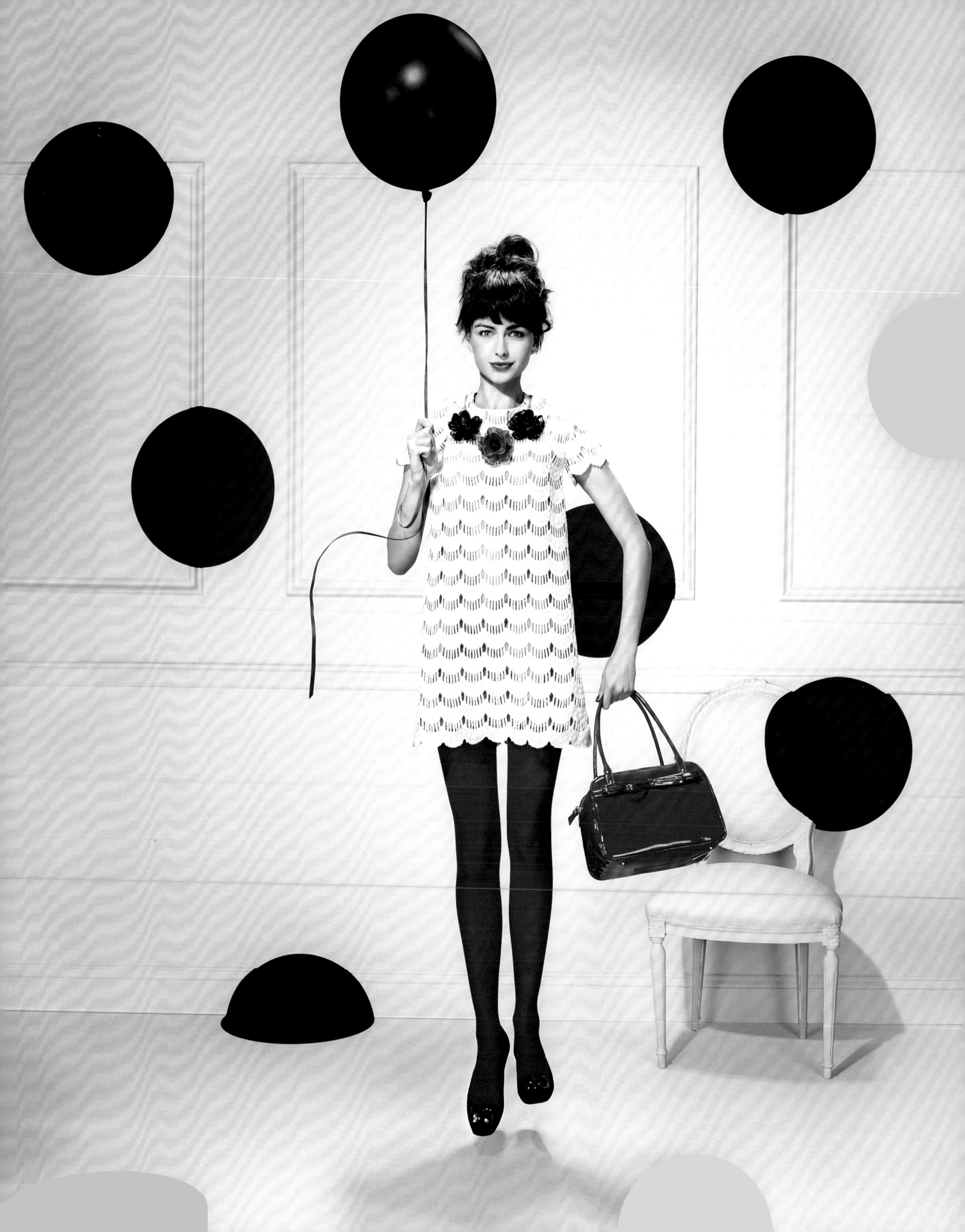

from a 2007 installation by artist felice varini at the musée des beaux-arts in arras, france. he is known for painting colorful fragments across vast, grand spaces, which, when viewed from a specific vantage point, create large geometric designs.

be dazzled by dots

*plan a trip to one of these permanent
exhibits to see the spot-on work of some of
our favorite artists.*

ARKEN MUSEUM OF MODERN ART
(near copenhagen) admire eight works
by british artist damien hirst, including his
largest spot painting to date.

THE MUSEUM OF MODERN ART
(new york) moma houses an impressive
collection of pop art by painter (and dot
devotee) roy lichtenstein.

VICTORIA AND ALBERT MUSEUM
(london) head to the ladies' loo for
a glimpse of felice varini's *six circles
in disorder*, which appears in its entirety
only by looking through the mirror.

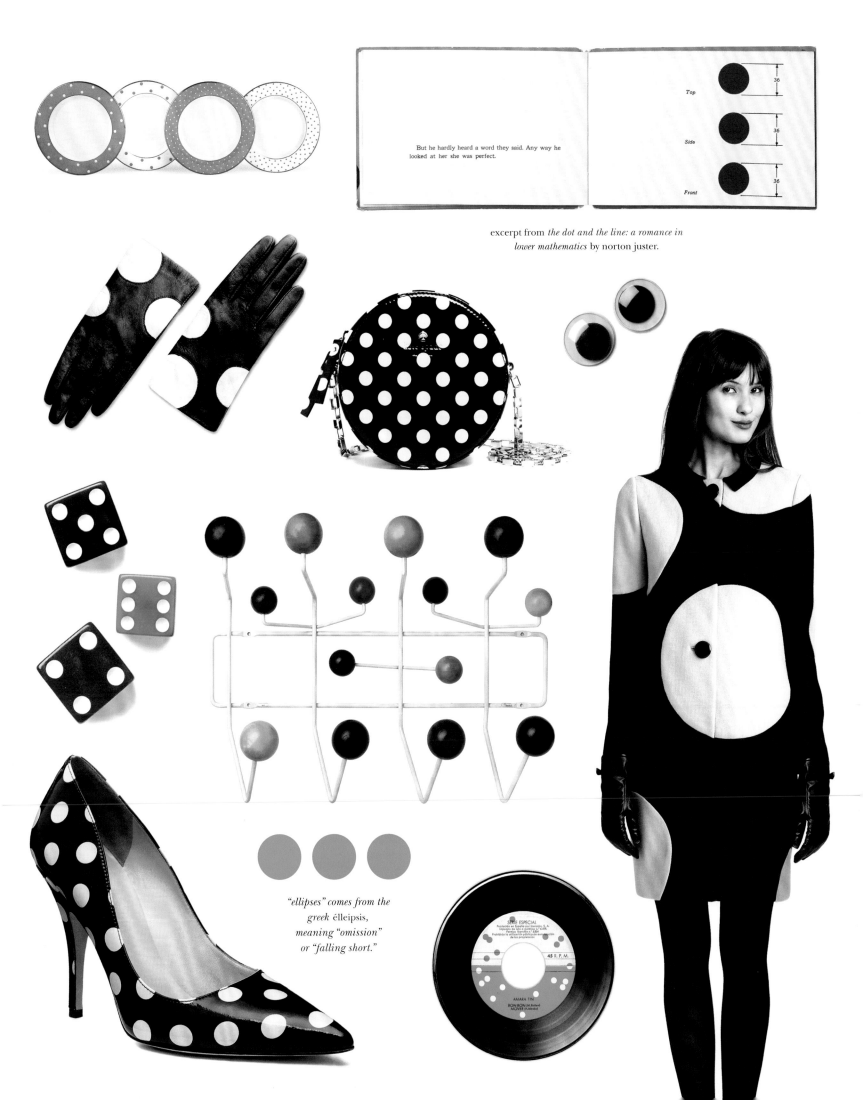

But he hardly heard a word they said. Any way he looked at her she was perfect.

Top 36

Side 36

Front 36

excerpt from *the dot and the line: a romance in lower mathematics* by norton juster.

"ellipses" comes from the greek élleipsis, meaning "omission" or "falling short."

everything starts
from a dot.

5

A
SENSE
OF
HUMOR

---

a sense of humor is key in all we do—
truly, this is a girl's best friend. in our
office, laughter rings out at regular
intervals and we admire women who
don't take themselves too seriously.

we love to design products with
funny little details and we're fond of
slipping favorite turns of phrase into
unexpected places. we're inspired by
famously clever characters like miranda
july and dorothy parker, who sums up
our philosophy perfectly: "take care
of the luxuries and the necessities will
take care of themselves."

we've compiled a collection of prose
by quick-witted wordsmiths who strike
our fancy. take a peek…

"i don't deserve any credit for turning the other cheek as my [...] fools—self-confidence my friends will call it." **EDGAR ALLAN POE**

most of my parentheses out, so as not to call undue attentio[n...] that i think only in short fragments or long, run-on though[ts...] to think of as disdain for the finality of the period)." **SARAH VOW[ELL]**

wherever she went, including here, it was against her better [...] and i was very flattered. but i was not pleased to read the des[...] a wall.'" **ELEANOR ROOSEVELT** "a dame that knows the ropes isn't lik[e...] again. then quit. there's no use being a damn fool about it." **W[...]**

somebody turns it on, i go into the library and read a good [...] sleep or pee or roll around on top of the other dogs. this one [...] pressed against the glass, looking at us with an extremely se[...] me to be saying, 'i am a sacred cow. get out your wallet.'" **A[...]**

emotional comfort, it was our belief that no amount of phy[...] cocktail." **DAVID SEDARIS** "that is my problem with life, i rush th[...] is slowness, like drinking relaxing tea. when i drink relaxing te[a...] tea the quickest." **MIRANDA JULY** "the most wasted of all days is [...] you miss all the fun." **KATHARINE HEPBURN** "a day without sunshi[ne...] again, i'd make the same mistakes, only sooner." **TALLULAH BAN[KHEAD]**

time. this was before i came to understand that you cannot [...] do. by arguing and pleading and screaming and crying an[d...] and sending flowers and buying gifts and doing unsolicit[ed...] declaring your abiding love and trying hard or sometimes [...] hitherto lukewarm really detest you." **PATRICIA MARX** "i have of[...] thinking about myself." **EDITH SITWELL** "i love deadlines. i love [...]

ngue is always in it." FLANNERY O'CONNOR "i have great faith in

have similar affection for the parenthesis (but i always take

to the glaring fact that i cannot think in complete sentences,

elays that the literati call stream of consciousness but i like

LL "that would be a good thing for them to cut on my tombstone:

dgment." DOROTHY PARKER "i once had a rose named after me

iption in the catalogue: 'no good in a bed, but fine up against

y to get tied up." MAE WEST "if at first you don't succeed, try, try

FIELDS "i must say i find television very educational. the minute

ook." GROUCHO MARX "normally, puppies in pet store windows

gnored its window-mates and was instead sitting with its nose

us little expression on its face. an expression that seemed to

GUSTEN BURROUGHS "we were not a hugging people. in terms of

ical contact could match the healing powers of a well-made

ugh it, like i'm being chased. even things whose whole point

i suck it down as if i'm in a contest for who can drink relaxing

ne without laughter." E. E. CUMMINGS "if you obey all the rules,

e is like, you know, night." STEVE MARTIN "if i had to live my life

EAD "if only, i thought, i could talk to eugene just one more

nake someone fall in love with you. but here's what you can

throwing plates and phoning a lot and bringing hot food

favors and remembering a birthday and being nice and

merely by being present, you can make someone who was

n wished i had time to cultivate modesty … but i am too busy

he whooshing noise they make as they go by." DOUGLAS ADAMS

6

SUMMER

there's a thrill of anticipation as the end of spring nears. it's an energy that charges the air as layers unpeel, shoulders are bared and pedicured toes tap happily in strappy sandals. summer is, without question, our favorite time of the year—giving us more excuses to entertain and more opportunities to stay out late and bask in the glow. even the sun lingers a bit longer in the sky during those hot summer months. the vibe is carefree and easy. sundresses are in season, freckles come out to play and the topknot is the hairstyle de rigueur.

SWAN DIVE
OR CANNONBALL?

the ubiquitous pink flamingo was invented by don featherstone in 1957.

style legend babe paley soaks in the sun in
her signature elegant style.

another unmistakable sign of summer: the
gently folding banana leaf print on this page.
named martinique, it was designed for the
beverly hills hotel by decorator don loper in
1942 and is one of the most iconic wallpapers
ever created.

astroturf was invented in 1964 and sold under the name chemgrass. it was renamed in 1966 after being installed in the houston astrodome.

"SHALL I COMPARE THEE TO A SUMMER'S DAY?"

WILLIAM SHAKESPEARE

"summer afternoon — summer afternoon … the two most beautiful words in the english language." **HENRY JAMES**

our high-school reading list
(worth revisiting)

emma by jane austen
jane eyre by charlotte brontë
wuthering heights by emily brontë
a tale of two cities by charles dickens
great expectations by charles dickens
robinson crusoe by daniel defoe
rebecca by daphne du maurier
the great gatsby by f. scott fitzgerald
to kill a mockingbird by harper lee
moby-dick by herman melville
1984 by george orwell
the catcher in the rye by j. d. salinger
romeo and juliet by william shakespeare
frankenstein by mary shelley
gulliver's travels by jonathan swift
the importance of being earnest by oscar wilde

*sunglasses are also known
as shades, spekkies, glecks, glints
and glares. our favorite
optical term of endearment is sunnies.*

fireflies use their lights to attract mates: among some species, the most successful suitors have the brightest flashes.

7

A POP
OF
COLOR

a pop of color has the power to punctuate an otherwise ordinary setting and can make for a far grander gesture than an overstated splash. think of a yellow umbrella on a gray day, a red dress in a sea of dark suits or glossy green heels peeking out from beneath a pair of navy trousers.

we channel this same spirit in our designs: giving a sophisticated work tote a colorful lining or selecting hot pink stitching to finish a basic pair of blue jeans. it's these little bright spots that bring a cheerful optimism to the items they accompany, and while they may seem serendipitous, they're often the result of great attention to detail. when seeking the perfect pop, what is taken away is just as important as what is left behind.

girls in the windows, photographed by
ormond gigli in new york city in 1960.
he staged the shot a day before these
brownstones—across the street from his
studio on 58th street—were razed.

polaroids from artist grant hamilton's *spectrum*, 2008, shot from one pack of film in a single day.

add a pop to your winter wardrobe
bring a favorite coat to the tailor and have it relined in a colorful print or fabric (we've found satin works best).

"THINK PINK!"

KAY THOMPSON

funny face

a welcome surprise: finding a flood of
cheerful color in a freshly opened letter.

at right: the lobby of the greenbrier resort
in white sulphur springs, west virginia,
decorated by the legendary dorothy draper
in 1946.

"i like the sudden shock of non-sequitur color." **BABE PALEY**

"color possesses me. i don't have to pursue it. color and i are one." **PAUL KLEE**

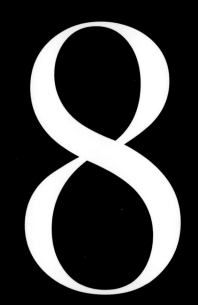

BLACK
AND
WHITE

we have a definitive point of view, and there's certainly no gray area when it comes to black and white. crisp and classic with a graphic sensibility, it's always pure and never shy. we're forever fans of the black-and-white stripe—whether on a handbag or in a home (let's not forget the impossibly chic *cour d'honneur* at paris's palais royal). we love the romantic nostalgia of movies like *casablanca* and *band of outsiders* and the enduringly modern appeal of black-and-white photography. a handsome stranger in a tailored black-and-white tuxedo has a knee-weakening effect, and a zebra-print rug pops in most any living space. as a color combination, it's simply one of the best. striking in its simplicity, it never fails to make a sharp first impression.

charcoal drawings from robert longo's famous *men in the cities* series, 1979.

BLACK AND
WHITE IS
ALWAYS RIGHT.

SIMPLY CLASSIC.

THE <u>REAL</u> JAMES DEAN

2/-

STORY

unlike the guests at his black-and-white ball, who spent handfuls of money on their one-of-a-kind masks, truman capote bought his at f.a.o. schwarz for thirty-nine cents.

dalmatians are born all white and develop spots as they grow.

legendary fashion photographer cecil
beaton, sitting in a sea of his portraits
of celebrities and society swans.

the rules of dominoes

cast in classic black and white, it's hands-down the chicest game we've found. here are the how-tos of a classic draw game: you'll need a double-six set and a partner to play.

shuffle the tiles facedown. each player draws seven dominoes and sets them on their sides. to begin, the first person places a domino of her choosing faceup on the table. this starts the line of play—a series of dominoes formed by matching the number of dots against each other. the players alternately extend the line of play at both ends. when one person cannot play from her hand, she must draw another domino. the game ends when the winner plays her final domino (and toasts with a white russian or a dark and stormy).

ACCESSORIZING
WITH
ABANDON

we're not shy about our penchant for statement pieces. after all, we believe that more is more and minimalism is, quite frankly, a bore. we admire the spirited aesthetic of women like iris apfel and diana vreeland and appreciate the over-the-top styling of a great fashion campaign.

we've long applied the philosophy of accessorizing with abandon to our personal sense of style. why wear one bangle when you could wear two (or three, or four)? why limit sparkles to your jewelry when you can add them to your shoes?

true, there's such a thing as excess— but we also believe there's an exception to every rule. so, if the cocktail ring fits, why not wear one in every color?

model jean shrimpton in 1970 posing
with items to be sold at auction, including
a hat worn by mae west, john lennon's
white oxford shirt and a cigarette holder
carried by claudia cardinale in the film
the pink panther.

NAME
iris barrel apfel

OCCUPATION
accessory designer

MANTRA
"fashion you can buy—but style you must possess." quote from edna woolman chase, i think.

STYLE INSPIRATION
life itself. it's so full of so many wondrous things and i muddle through it sopping up everything like a giant sponge.

MY MOTHER TAUGHT ME
to worship at the altar of the accessory.

TO ME, ACCESSORIZING IS
transformative.

MY FAVORITE SPLURGE OF ALL TIME
a magnificent period brooch—the turbaned head of a blackamoor set with tiny seventeenth-century cameos—made by codognato.

DRESSING UP MEANS
an adrenaline rush.

WHEN ALL ELSE FAILS
try again! it's an ancient adage, but there is nothing more corny than the truth.

CURIOSITY IS
my life's blood.

I KEEP MY BEST PIECES
ready to wear!

OF ALL MY TRAVELS, I'VE BEEN MOST INFLUENCED BY
everything!!!!

MY GREATEST FASHION COUP
my first exhibition at the metropolitan museum of art's costume institute, called *rara avis*, in september 2005.

THE ONE THING I CONTINUE TO SEARCH FOR
peace of mind.

IRIS APFEL
a dossier on the doyenne of personal style.

10

THE
CHA-CHA

---

whether you know the steps or admire the moves from afar, the cha-cha has an infectious quality to it. the word itself is fun to say, like so many moves from eras past—watusi, anyone?

we love the cha-cha in practice—and as art. andy warhol's early dance steps inspired a slew of graphics that we've used in our shops and played with on our products. we're endlessly inspired by the covers of vintage vinyls that we seek out at flea markets and find in thrift stores (over the years, we've built quite the collection).

it's a nondiscriminating dance. you can cha-cha to the classics or cha-cha to beyoncé. it's sexy but demure—and so simple to pick up, we've taught it to party guests at different events around the world.

it's an old-school reference that's still irresistibly fun. to quote truvy in *steel magnolias,* "it's too cha-cha for words."

AMBO, A CHA-CHA AI

Ritmando

Malagueña

La Violettera

Ahora Seremos Felices

Un Malagueño in Paris

Qué Mentirosa

Estrellita

La Conga Sevillana

OPICANA ORCHESTR

Alminana Soler, Con

EREOPHONIC

45-C

SOL

CHA!
CHA
CHA
CHA CHA

SCORE! RECORDS
CHA CHA

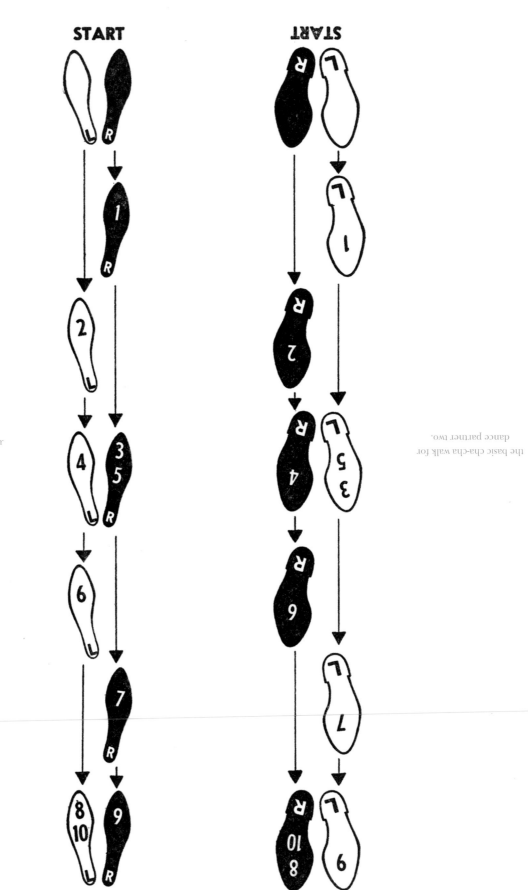

the basic cha-cha walk for
dance partner one.

the basic cha-cha walk for
dance partner two.

"DANCE, DANCE, DANCE TILL YOU DROP."

W. H. AUDEN

A CHA-CHA TIMELINE

late 1940s
cuban composer enrique jorrín creates a new,
easier-to-dance-to twist on the mambo.

1952–53
dancers at havana's silver star club shimmy
to the tunes and spin them into a new style
of dancing named for the shuffling *cha cha cha*
sound their feet make on the dance floor.

1954
the infectious one-two, one-two-three rhythm sparks
a cha-cha craze that spreads to the u.s.

1955
pérez prado's cha-cha tune, "cherry
pink and apple blossom white," hits number
one on the american pop charts.

1957
cha-cha contagion carries over to tv, where
american bandstand coins the "chalypso"—its name
for the teen version of the cha-cha...

1964
bollywood is hit with cha-cha fever,
making films like *cha cha cha*.

1978
the country goes wild for the film *grease*,
including a cameo by the oh-so-memorable "cha cha,"
who almost steals danny from under sandy's nose
with her dance moves.

2009
kate spade new york kicks off a fashion's
night out fête with in-store cha-cha lessons (the first
of many cha-cha shindigs to come...).

dr. no

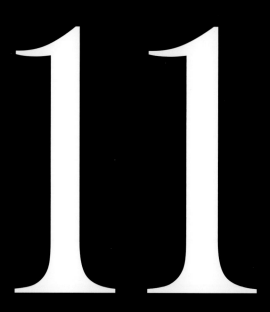

11

THE
CINEMA

we're constantly inspired by the spirit of the cinema. we embrace the chance to escape—if only for a few hours—to a faraway adventure (or simply an air-conditioned seat on a hot summer day). whether you're settling into a plush velvet seat or catching a special screening of *the thomas crown affair* at the drive-in, there's a feeling of festivity about seeing a film.

and the trappings of cinema are just as enchanting: those opening title sequences (of which saul bass is king), well-styled sets, wardrobes that steal the show and clever turns of phrase effortlessly delivered by an especially charming actor all prove that often the plot is (almost) beside the point.

breakfast at tiffany's

left to right, top to bottom: willy wonka and the chocolate factory, a woman is a woman, the graduate, breathless, the royal tenenbaums, charade, the man with the

golden arm, pierrot le fou, in the mood for love, who are you, polly maggoo?, the red balloon, love story, bonnie and clyde, sixteen candles, cleo from 5 to 7.

This poetic decadence is awful...

"FILM IS MAINLY RHYTHM; IT IS INHALATION AND EXHALATION IN CONTINUOUS SEQUENCE."

INGMAR BERGMAN

BEAUTIFUL
TYPE

defined as the way letters appear on a page, typography is an art.

as a brand that prizes the power of the written word, we believe the type is as vital as the ink. when treated right, a single word—the punctuation, even—can become a miniature masterpiece. and often, for us, it does.

we find type to be irresistibly sexy. we love superthin serifs mingled with bold stems and the voluptuous curves of a perfect *o*. we've been known to swipe a particularly lovely business card for the singular purpose of lusting over its typography.

achieving the perfect balance when setting type is often like walking a tightrope. it must be complementary but not consuming. the right font adds flavor to the message it communicates; it can be playful, charming, bold or timid. it speaks a universal language. even if the subject matter is written in greek, typography can translate its intent simply in the movement of its lines (or lack thereof).

LE CORBUSIER

FUTURA

BODONI

*we appreciate beautiful type in so many mediums. it adds an artful element to our
"pardon my french" bangle and question mark clutch. it can make a book cover instantly
elegant and a business card irresistible. we're especially fond of futura, bodoni and
le corbusier. (this caption is written in baskerville italics, in case you were wondering.)*

BAZ AR

PER'S

HAR V

34 NEW
SCHEMES FOR
THE SOUTH

LATE NEWS
FOR LEGS:
THE
SHIMMERING
STOCKINGS

GIFTS: THE
THOUGHT IS
THE THING

"EACH LETTER SHOULD HAVE A FLIRTATION WITH THE ONE NEXT TO IT."

MAC BAUMWELL

happy, a 1999 light installation by british
artists tim noble and sue webster.

13

AN
ELEMENT
OF
SURPRISE

we delight in the unexpected details. skywriting, snowmen in the city, a wayward bunch of balloons—each has the ability to surprise and prompt a smile. we appreciate them when we come across them by chance, and we love to slip them into our products.

to celebrate the launch of our flagship shop in tokyo, we covered it in hundreds of pinwheels, giving passersby a spirited hello. our colorful idiom bangles feature a tiny turn of phrase delicately inscribed inside, so that it's as if you're wearing a secret on your wrist. we particularly enjoy those sartorial sleights of hand that make us do a double take: an over-the-top accessory fashioned from an everyday object or a straw hat with inset shades that makes an oversize disguise for the eyes (simply pull it down lower and enjoy spying on the sly).

it's the pursuit of these twists that keeps us on our toes. what's next, you ask? you won't be stunned to hear… it's a surprise!

make someone's day: pay the valet for the car after yours.

*a menagerie of our most-loved fashion surprises, including
a trompe l'oeil minaudière that masquerades as a rolled-up magazine
and a miniaturized elephant made into a summer accent.*

EAT CAKE FOR BREAK-FAST.

play doorbell ditch, leaving a clever keepsake at a friend's doorstep.

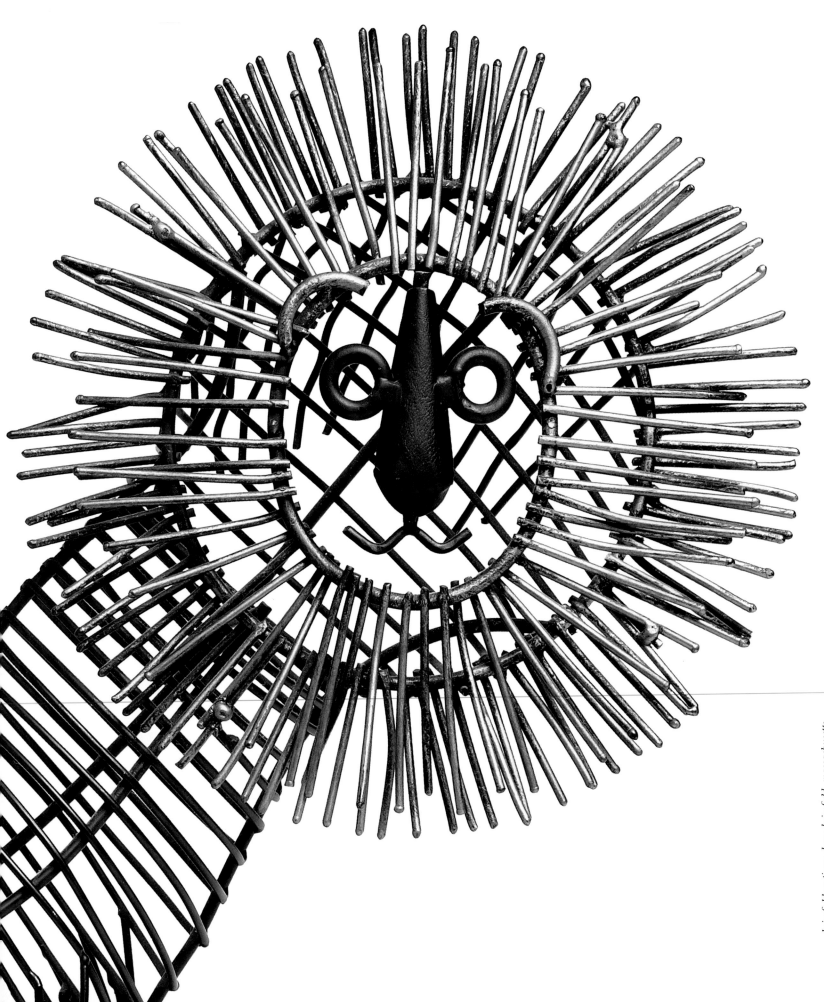

14

FLEA
MARKET
FINDS

---

our original offices were nestled in a manhattan neighborhood known for its vintage shops—and this didn't happen by chance. vintage shopping, antiquing and all-around treasure hunting has always been a favorite pastime. the pure thrill of the chase has motivated many an early morning of flea marketing, both in the city and around the world.

there's no telling what you'll find on any given day. there have been afternoons where we've come home empty-handed and then there have been times when we've found things beyond our wildest dreams (deborah lloyd, an avid art collector, once discovered a man ray sketch while browsing the brooklyn flea).

from buckets and bins filled to the brim with bejeweled accessories to vintage prints and hand-stitched garments—the likes of which you won't find anywhere else—our flea market finds tend to prove that one person's trash really is another's treasure.

maxwell street market, chicago, illinois.

alameda point antique fair, alameda, california.

A TROVE OF OUR MOST TREASURED FINDS.

yard sale, topeka, kansas.

portobello road, london.

brooklyn flea, brooklyn, new york.

26th street flea, new york, new york.

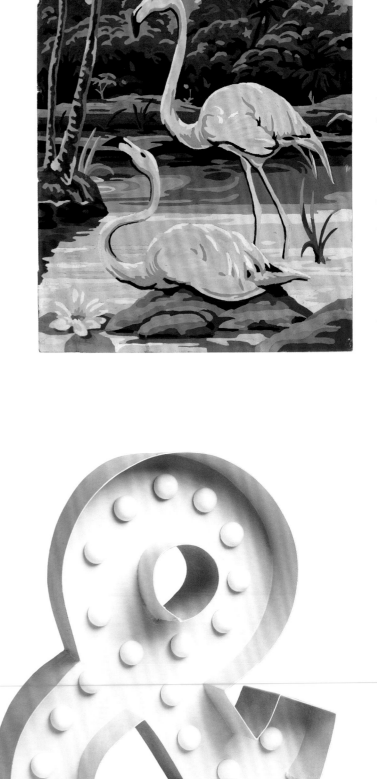

renningers, mount dora, florida.

shupp's grove antique market, adamstown, pennsylvania.

les puces de saint-ouen, paris.

the emporium, frederick, maryland.

rose bowl flea market, pasadena, california.

15

whether it's a daredevil stunt, like piloting a plane that's never been flown before, or an improvised journey, like taking your niece on the tram to roosevelt island because she thinks it's a flying train, adventures remind us that we're alive and make even ordinary destinations seem grander.

we relish the nostalgic tug of escapades from years gone by—take building tree houses or playing hooky (which we're still known to do on occasion). it's the thrill of adventure that makes us love the precipitous dive of a roller coaster and inspires the wanderlust that takes us away each summer.

whether we're taking flight to faraway locales or escaping right in our own hometowns, it's these journeys that illuminate every day, and awaken us with a jolt to life's breathtaking possibilities.

our road trip playlist

tried-and-true tunes for long drives

HOLD ON TIGHT electric light orchestra

CALIFORNIA STARS billy bragg and wilco

ALRIGHT supergrass

SLIPPIN' AND SLIDIN' otis redding

THE PASSENGER iggy pop

(I'M A) ROAD RUNNER junior walker and the all stars

PHOTOGRAPH astrud gilberto

TWO OF US the beatles

TAKE IT EASY jackson browne

HOMEWARD BOUND simon & garfunkel

INTO THE GREAT WIDE OPEN tom petty

BORN TO BE WILD steppenwolf

CITY OF NEW ORLEANS arlo guthrie

TILL THE END OF THE DAY the kinks

STARMAN david bowie

ISLAND IN THE SUN weezer

our ship clutch was inspired by one of our favorite types of wanderlust: the ocean voyage.

model lisa fonssagrives falling through the
sky in a pair of elsa schiaparelli pajamas.
considered to be the first supermodel
by many, the swedish-born beauty (who
also appears on the previous page of this
book) was quite fearless when it came to
getting a great photograph, as evidenced
by this photo.

"ONE'S
DESTINATION
IS NEVER A PLACE
BUT RATHER
A NEW WAY OF
LOOKING
AT THINGS."

HENRY MILLER

MOST
LIKELY TO
★ ★ ★
BUY A
ONE-WAY
TICKET

"pleasure to me is wonder—the unexplored, the unexpected . . ." **H. P. LOVECRAFT**

16

ALL
THAT
GLITTERS

---

understated is overrated. we've found that sparkle is not for the faint of heart—or shy of style. it's an especially festive factor for those who choose to dabble in it, guaranteeing a few head turns (and perhaps even a cocktail or two, compliments of the gentleman at the bar).

gold, in particular, is our favorite glittery go-to. we see it as our sassy neutral, a hue too chic to hold court on the color wheel. its allure is nothing to take lightly: its gleam has long lured explorers to new destinations and its spellbinding powers are legend. yet, despite its dazzling appeal, it plays well with others, working with every ensemble and giving even the most basic pieces a lift.

during the empire state building's recent renovation, artisans used 23-carat gold and more than 115,000 sheets of aluminum leaf to restore the lobby's gilded ceiling mural.

"*I WANTED ALL TO SPARKLE, AND DANCE IN A GLORIOUS JUBILEE.*"

EMILY BRONTË
wuthering heights

see how they sparkle

some of the very best vantage points for
viewing skylines around the world

NEW YORK
the roof garden café and martini bar
at the metropolitan museum of art

ATHENS
rooftop garden at the plaka hotel

PARIS
sacré-coeur basilica

TOKYO
the peak bar at the park hyatt hotel

STOCKHOLM
gondolen restaurant

SEOUL
namsan tower

LOS ANGELES
the top of runyon canyon

LONDON
portrait restaurant at the national
portrait gallery

SHANGHAI
the 88th floor of the jin mao tower

17

HANDWRITTEN NOTES

in the age of e-mails, texts and tweets, there's something irresistibly charming about receiving a personal letter in the mail. it's a rarity, to be sure, the result of extra effort and attention to detail. these days, when everything is digital and relatively uniform in its appearance, a handwritten note stands out as all the more notable.

from the words you use to the paper—and even the ink—you choose, each element makes a statement and says a little something about the message you send. we opt for handwritten notes when it comes to birthday cards and thank-yous, but they're often most appreciated when they're completely unexpected: a post-it note hello, stuck someplace inconspicuous; an invitation for impromptu cocktails delivered via paper airplane; or a quick love note scrawled in the steam on the bathroom mirror always imparts extra delight.

It's so damned
good to
occasionally
find courage
and good taste
combined —

**correspondence that's
best written by hand**

general invitations
wedding invitations
birth announcements
thank-you notes
moving announcements
"dear john" letters
place cards
love letters
vacation postcards
fan mail

dana—
there is a bottle of wine
under my desk for later.
—Katie

the long and the short of it

Small card. Big thank you.

How the devil are you?

99 thank yous

MGB

watch less, write more

COFFEE?
3:00?
YAY   NAY

-JOHN

"you can't reread a telephone call." LIZ CARPENTER

18

COCKTAILS

this chapter is a celebration of libations.

it won't come as a surprise that we've picked cocktails as one of our favorite things. from cocktail rings to cocktail hours, everything about the word buzzes with a festive spirit.

we love the names of classic drinks— the sloe gin fizz, singapore sling or boston sidecar—and the old-school lounges and bars where they were served. we love giving said drinks a modern-day twist and perfecting our pours with elegant glassware and playful accoutrements (a circus-stripe straw, say).

a cocktail party is the perfect excuse to get dressed up and mingle—whether you're meeting new people or simply enjoying time with old friends. and let's not forget cocktail conversation; it's frequently the most fascinating part of the evening.

ABSINTHE DRIP ADMIRAL AFTER SIX ALABAMA SLAMMER
BEAUTY AMERICANO HIGHBALL ANGEL'S KISS ANN SH
ANESTHETIC AVIATION BACKSEAT BOOGIE BAHAMA MAM
BARBARY COAST BELLAMY SCOTCH SOUR BERMUDA ROS
MAGIC BLACKOUT BLACK VELVET BLESSED EVENT BLINK
BOURBON SOCIETY BRANDY CAPRICE BRANDY SMASH BRAS
CARROT CAKE CASABLANCA CASINO CHAMPAGNE PU
COCOBANANA COMMANDO COOPERSTOWN CORONATION
CUPID'S CORNER DARK AND STORMY DEATH IN THE AFTE
FIZZ DICK AND JANE DIPLOMAT DUPLEX EAGLE EDITH I
FORTRESS FOG CUTTER FOREIGN AFFAIR FOUR HORSEMEN
GIN AND TONIC GIN DAISY GIN SLING GOLDEN CADILLAC
HABANEROS HANKY PANKY HARVEY WALLBANGER HAT T
BUTTERED RUM HOT TODDY HURRICANE JACK ROSE JA
KANGAROO KICKER KIR ROYALE KNICKERBOCKER LANCER
BLUSH MAMIE TAYLOR MANHATTAN MARTINI MARY PIC
MICKEY SLIM MIDNIGHT JOY MILLIONAIRE MINT JULEP M
MOSCOW MULE MR. NEW YORKER NAKED WAITER NAPO
FASHIONED OLYMPIA ORANGE BLOSSOM ORCHID PALMET
PER F'AMOUR PICK ME UP PIMM'S CUP PINK LADY PLANTER
PURPLE HAZE RAMOS FIZZ RED LOTUS REMSEN COOLER I
HIGHBALL ROMAN PUNCH ROSE ROUND ROBIN ROYAL I
DOG SANGAREE SANGRIA SANTIAGO SAVOY AFFAIR SAZER
MORN SHADY LADY SHAMROCK SHERRY FLIP SHOOTING
ROYALE SLOE GIN RICKEY SNOWBALL SNOW WHITE SOO
HIGHBALL ST. CHARLES PUNCH STINGER SUNDOWNE
MODERNISTA TOM AND JERRY TOM COLLINS TRINITY T
WALDORF WHISKEY SOUR WHITE RUSSIAN WHIZZ BANG

LEXANDER THE GREAT ALL-AMERICAN PUNCH AMERICAN
RIDAN APPLEJACK ARCH OF TRIUMPH ASTOR PAINLESS
BAHAMAS HIGHBALL BALLET RUSSE BALTIMORE EGGNOG
BETWEEN-THE-SHEETS BIJOU BLACKBERRY PUNCH BLACK
R BLOODY MARY BLUE BLAZER BOOMERANG BOSSA NOVA
MONKEY BRONX BROOKLYNITE BUTTERFLY CAFE DE PARIS
CH CLAM DIGGER CLARET LEMONADE CLOVER CLUB
ORPSE REVIVER COTILLION CUBA LIBRE CUFF & BUTTONS
OON DEBUTANTE'S DREAM DERBY DEVIL'S TAIL DIAMOND
Y EL PRESIDENTE EYE-OPENER FELLINI FLIRTINI FLYING
FRENCH 75 FRISCO FROZEN DAIQUIRI FULL MOON GIMLET
OLDEN GATE GOLDEN SLIPPER GRASSHOPPER GREENBRIER
ICK HAWAII HOCUS-POCUS HONEY BEE HONEYMOON HOT
ED LADY JAMAICA RUM JOHN COLLINS JULIUS SPECIAL
RANC LEMON DROP LONDON CALLING LORRAINE MAIDEN'S
XFORD MATADOR MEMPHIS BELLE MERRY WIDOW MIAMI
SSOURI MULE MOJITO MOONWALK MORNING GLORY FIZZ
ON NATIONAL NEW ORLEANS FIZZ NIAGARA FALLS OLD-
O PANAMA PARADISE PARISIAN PARKEROO PEACH VELVET
S PUNCH POMPIER HIGHBALL PORT FLIP PURPLE EMPEROR
AD RUNNER ROB ROY ROCKY MOUNTAIN COOLER ROMAN
ZZ RUBY DUTCHESS RUM SCOUNDREL RUSTY NAIL SALTY
C SCHNORKEL SCOTCH COOLER SEA BREEZE SEPTEMBER
TAR SIDECAR SILK STOCKING SINGAPORE SLING SLAMMER
ETY SOUTH OF THE BORDER SOUTH SIDE FIZZ SPRITZER
SWISS YODELER THE BUSINESS THE GODFATHER THE
OPICAL LIFE SAVER VENUS DE MILO VICTORY VOLCANO
ILDFLOWER WOO WOO YELLOW PARROT ZOMBIE ZOOM

a toast in a pinch...

here's to _____.
                (noun)

my _____ _____, who _____
   (adjective) (relationship)   (achievement)

may you _____ with _____
          (verb)   (noun)

and _____ _____ _____.
    (frequency) (verb) (noun)

cheers!

STORK CLUB

MOST
LIKELY TO
_____
ORDER
ANOTHER
ROUND

our gleaming ring pouch (above) keeps
hands festive and free to clink,
while the toast-worthy clutch below is topped
with a lucite "ice cube" clasp. cheers!

our colorful coasters make a spirited
addition to any celebration.

DOWN THE HATCH

ON THE ROCKS

WITH A TWIST

MARTINI

INGREDIENTS

1 OUNCE DRY GIN

¼ OUNCE DRY VERMOUTH

¼ OUNCE ITALIAN VERMOUTH

WEDGE OF LEMON

PREPARATION

STIR WELL IN CRUSHED ICE

RUB RIM OF FROSTED GLASS WITH LE

STRAIN DRINK INTO GLASS AND SE

bottoms up

kate spade
NEW YORK

COCKTAIL
COLORFULLY

kate spade
NEW YORK

*"i love a martini—but two
at the most. three, i'm under the table;
four, i'm under the host."*

DOROTHY PARKER

POP
FIZZ
CLINK

"TOO MUCH OF
ANYTHING IS BAD,
BUT TOO MUCH
CHAMPAGNE
IS JUST RIGHT."

MARK TWAIN

19

BOLD
BLOOMS

we love florals—with a twist. historically, flowers have been admired for their soft femininity, graceful silhouettes and delicate fragrance. while we appreciate these sweet attributes, we're particularly partial to florals that truly pop (after all, there are no wallflowers here).

in our products, we'll never let the bloom fall off the rose, so to speak. by saturating a floral in a fluorescent hue, or elevating a single bloom to epic proportions (on a cocktail ring for instance), a bashful blossom becomes a striking statement. it's these twists that make things more interesting and lead to our favorite types of florals: the ones that seem to beckon "pick me!"

"everything is blooming most recklessly."
RAINER MARIA RILKE

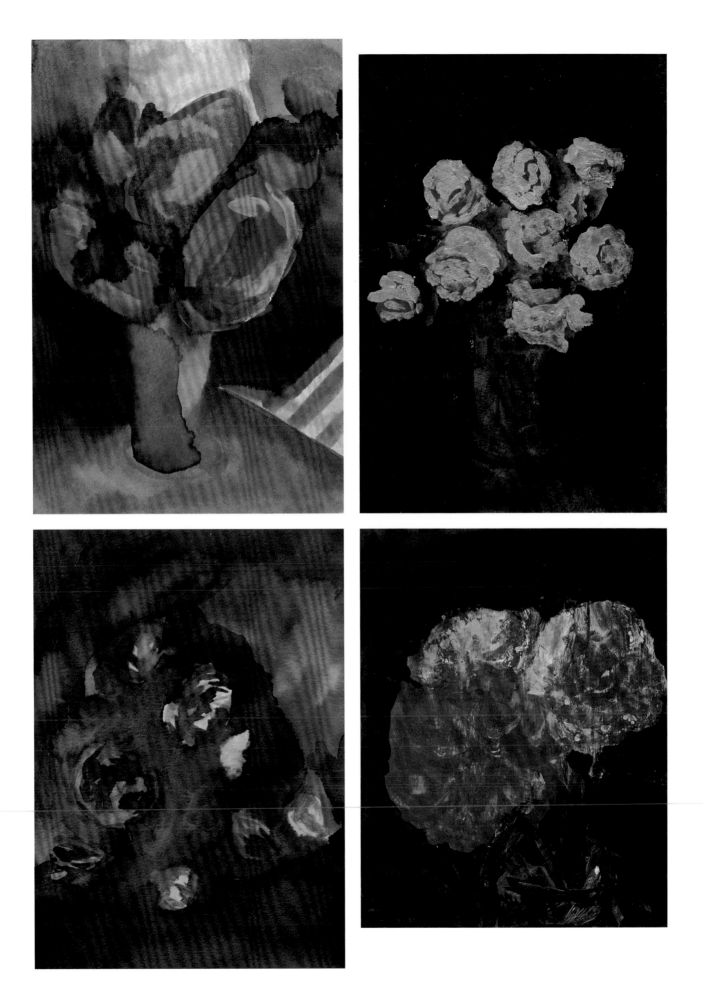

a collection of fetching floral paintings by the artist leanne shapton. clockwise from top left:
valentine roses (2007), *glowing flowers* (2006), *after fantin-latour 2* (2006), *pink flowers* (2006).

SHE'S NO SHRINKING VIOLET.

———

"earth laughs in flowers."
RALPH WALDO EMERSON

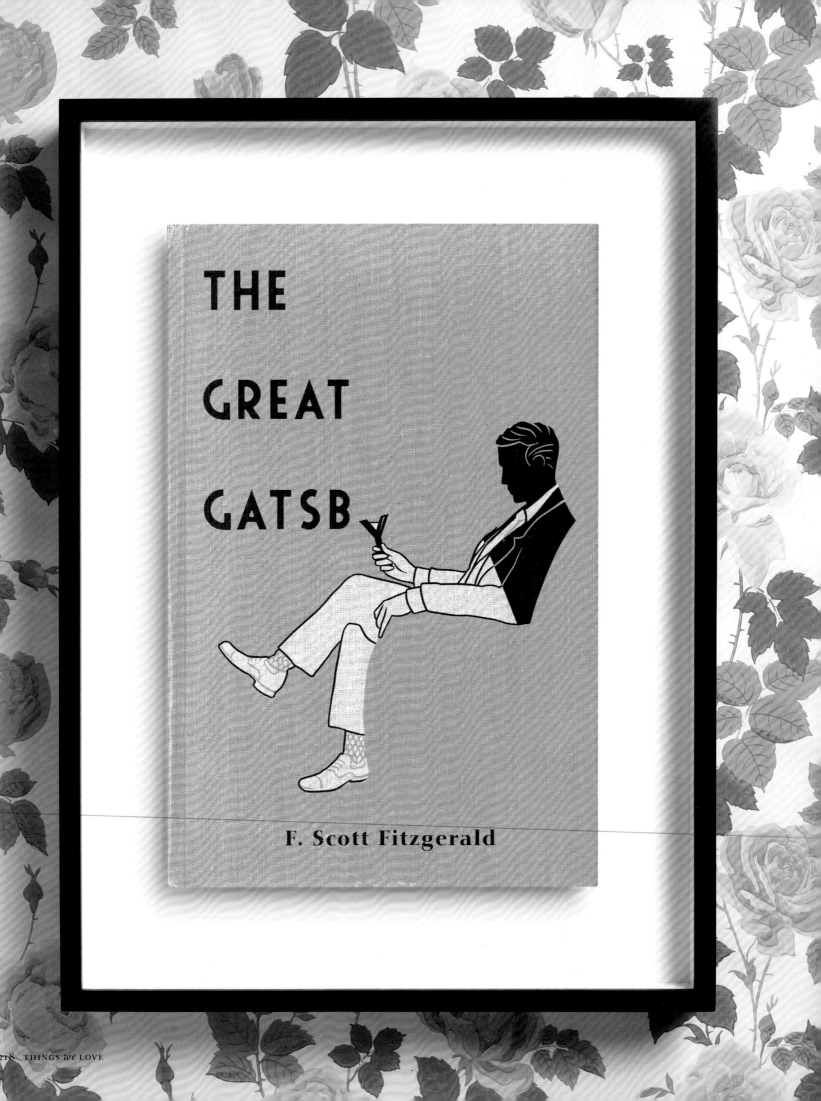

BOOKS

judge a book by its cover? absolutely. while we love books for the tales they tell, we'll admit to being swayed by a particularly sassy spine, brilliant title or beautiful cover. we once curated a show at colette in paris, "an argument for looking at books instead of reading them." this literary exhibit traveled from our new york showrooms to japan and finally france, paying tribute to a collection of striking, unusual book jackets that included both secondhand works as well as rare first editions.

books are unique in that their small size can downplay their substance. you can travel to far-flung places through the pages of a book, fall in love with a character you'll remember forever or come across a story that will entirely change the way you view the world. to borrow the words of charles w. eliot, books are the quietest and most constant of friends—making for great company wherever we may wander.

turn a favorite title into fine art: we framed a copy of f. scott fitzgerald's most famous novel, making a graphic masterpiece from this classic read.

ch now and a...

ive deep in the drive, and alread...

e gaudy with primary colors, and hair shorn in s

shawls beyond the dreams of Castile. The bar is i

ng rounds of cocktails permeate the garden outside

ith chatter and laughter, and casual innuendo and

n on the spot, and enthusiastic meetings between

new each other's names.

lights grow brighter as the earth lurches away fro

he orchestra is playing yellow cocktail music, and t

tches a key higher. Laughter is easier minute by mi

digality, tipped out at a cheerful word. The groups c

swell with new arrivals, dissolve and form in the s

ere are wanderers, confident girls who weave here a

outer and more stable, become for a sharp, joyous m

group, and then, excited with triumph, glide on th

d olor under the constantly

bling op

a novel idea: we reimagined the covers of our favorite titles and
fashioned them into these clever clutches that should not be left on the shelf.

"I HAD ALWAYS IMAGINED PARADISE AS A KIND OF LIBRARY."

JORGE LUIS BORGES

**twenty colorful tomes
we always keep in our library**

a wonderful time
by slim aarons
beaton in the sixties
by cecil beaton
the long-winded lady
by maeve brennan
my life in france
by julia child
slouching towards bethlehem
by joan didion
tender is the night
by f. scott fitzgerald
the americans
by robert frank
the sun also rises
by ernest hemingway
then
by alexander liberman
atonement
by ian mcewan
one special summer
by jacqueline and lee bouvier
a time to be born
by dawn powell
them: a memoir of parents
by francine du plessix gray
franny and zooey
by j. d. salinger
on beauty
by zadie smith
the elements of style
by strunk and white
walden
by henry david thoreau
my life and hard times
by james thurber
allure
by diana vreeland
brideshead revisited
by evelyn waugh

sometimes books can steal the show, as in these stills from our short film "seven henrietta street."

SHE IS
QUICK
AND
CURIOUS
AND
PLAYFUL
AND
STRONG

A COLLECTION OF
SHORT STORIES

kate spade
NEW YORK

GO IN PEACE,
NOT IN PIECES
laurie baker

LOVE AND OTHER
CONVICTIONS
bridie clark

WAITING
amanda smyth

ENGAGEMENT
CHICKEN
hannah seligson

ANNA & PATRICK
ilana stanger-ross

GOOD-BYE, MY LADY
suzanne rivecca

GIRL 57
sara wilkomerson

18 MILES OF BOOKS
STRAND
NEW YORK CITY • EST. 1927

in 2010 we collaborated with legendary bookseller the strand to commission
a series of short novellas. to pique their imaginations, the authors were sent a
colorful phrase that captures the spirit of kate spade new york.

"THE WORLD
WAS HERS FOR
THE READING."

BETTY SMITH
a tree grows in brooklyn

THE END.

index
and
credits

1

2

3

4

5

6

7

8

9

10

11

12

1   (left): © Suza Scalora
    (right): © Lopert Pictures/Photofest

2   (left, red mobile): Alexander Calder, *Big Red*, 1959. Accession #61.46. © 2012 Calder Foundation, New York/Artists Rights Society (ARS), New York
    (right, red binoculars): Photograph by Johnny Miller
    (right, red typewriter): Courtesy of Aaron Dyer

3   © Tierney Gearon

4   (left): © René Gruau, renegruau.com
    (right, red Pantone chip): PANTONE Color identification is solely for artistic purposes and not intended to be used for specification. PANTONE and the Pantone Chip logo are trademarks of Pantone LLC in the United States and/or other countries. Produced with the permission of Pantone LLC

5   © Jaime Monfort/Getty Images

6   (right): © Philippe Halsmann/Magnum Photos

7   (left): © Koto Bolofo/Art Dept.
    (right): © Norman Parkinson Limited/courtesy Norman Parkinson Archive

9   (left/top left): © William Klein
    (left/top right): © Bud Fraker/Paramount/Courtesy of Blow-Up Archive
    (left/bottom left): Photograph by Tom Palumbo
    (left/bottom right): © Vernon Stratton/Hulton Archive/Getty Images
    (right): © Serge Leblon

10 From *What Shall I Wear: The What, Where, When and How Much of Fashion* by Claire McCardell. First published in 1956 by Simon & Schuster. New edition typography, design and layout copyright © 2012 The Rookery Press, New York, NY. All rights reserved

11 (right): © Elliot Erwitt/Magnum Photos

13

14

15

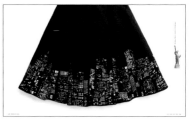

16

17

18

19

20

21

22

23

24

25

26

27

28

29

30

31

32

33

34

35

36

37

38

39

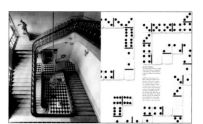

40

41

42

43

44

45   46   47   48

49   50   51   52

53   54   55   56

57   58   59   60

61 (right/top left): © Sahm Doherty/ Time & Life Pictures/Getty Images (right/top right): © Gordon Parks/ Time & Life Pictures/Getty Images (right/bottom left): Photograph by Jack Robinson, Condé Nast Archive (right/bottom right): © Robert Randall/Condé Nast Archive/CORBIS (left, bottom): Andrew Ingalls

62 © Tim Walker/Art + Commerce

65 (left): Courtesy of Aaron Dyer (right): *Slow* (Karin Mossberg, Nairobi/Kenya 1966). Photograph by F.C. Gundlach

66 © Lillian Bassman

67 (left): Dressed by Schiaparelli, Lisa Fonssagrives parachutes in Paris. Photograph by Jean Moral, 1937 © Brigitte Moral-Planté, Paris. Courtesy of Gitterman Gallery (right): © Koto Bolofo/Art Dept.

68 © Paramount Pictures/Photofest

69 (right): William Eggleston, *Untitled (Glass in Airplane)*, from the Los Alamos Portfolio, 1965–74. © Eggleston Artistic Trust. Courtesy of Cheim & Read, New York

70 (right): © Tim Walker/Art + Commerce

71 (left): © Tim Walker/Art + Commerce (right): © Altrendo Images/Getty Images

72 (left, book with gold vinyl letters): Abby Clawson Low of HI + LO

73 (left): © Momoko Takeda/ Getty Images (right): © Estate of Guy Bourdin. Reproduced by permission of Art + Commerce

74 (left): © Gordon Parks/Time & Life Pictures/Getty Images (right): Courtesy of Dana Lucas

77

78

79

80

81

82

83

84

85

86

87

88

89

90

sources

p016 calder quote: kuh, katharine. *the artist's voice: talks with seventeen modern artists.* boston, ma: da capo press, 2000.

p021 matisse quote: leland, nita. *confident color: an artist's guide to harmony, contrast and unity.* cincinnati, oh: north light books, 2008.

p022 blass quote: jarski, rosemarie. *words from the wise.* new york: skyhorse publishing, 2007.

p024 monroe quote: hutchinson, steve and helen lawrence. *playing with purpose: how experiential learning can be more than a game.* burlington, vt: gower publishing, 2011.

p032 saint laurent quote: "couture monday: yves saint laurent bow collection (ghosts of christmas makeup past, part 1)." *the makeup museum.* the makeup museum, 19 december 2011. web. 15 june 2012.

p042 de beauvoir quote: de beauvoir, simone. *america day by day.* trans. by carol cosman. berkeley, ca: university of california press, 2000.

p068 o'connor quote: o'connor, flannery. *the habit of being: letters of flannery o'connor.* ed. sally fitzgerald. new york: farrar, straus and giroux, 1979.

poe quote: poe, edgar allan. *the works of edgar allan poe: vol. iii, poems and essays.* ed. john h. ingram. 3rd edition. edinburgh: adam and charles black, 1883.

vowell quote: vowell, sarah. "dark circles." *take the cannoli: stories from the new world.* new york: simon & schuster, 2000.

parker quote: parker, dorothy. "but the one on the right." *the new yorker,* 19 oct. 1929: pg. 24.

roosevelt quote: brenner, douglas, and stephen scanniello. *a rose by any name: the little-known lore and deep-rooted history of rose names.* chapel hill, nc: algonquin books, 2009.

west quote: witchel, alex. "blown sideways, but landing on broadway." *new york times.* 8 may 2010, late ed., e1.

fields quote: shapiro, fred r. *the yale book of quotations.* new haven, ct: yale university press, 2006.

marx quote: shapiro, fred r. *the yale book of quotations.* new haven, ct: yale university press, 2006.

burroughs quote: burroughs, augusten. *possible side effects.* new york: picador, 2006.

sedaris quote: sedaris, david. *naked.* boston: little, brown and company, 1997.

july quote: july, miranda. *no one belongs here more than you.* new york: scriber, 2007.

cummings quote: "quote of the day." *the gazette.* montreal. august 2, 2011: a1.

hepburn quote: crimp, susan, comp. *katharine hepburn once said . . . : great lines to live by.* new york: harpercollins, 2003.

martin quote: jarski, rosemarie. *words from the wise.* new york: skyhorse publishing, 2007.

bankhead quote: sherrin, ned. *oxford dictionary of humorous quotations.* oxford: oxford university press, 2008.

marx quote: marx, patricia. *him her him again the end of him.* new york: scribner, 2007.

sitwell quote: sherrin, ned. *oxford dictionary of humorous quotations.* oxford: oxford university press, 2008.

adams quote: simpson, m. j. *hitchhiker: a biography of douglas adams.* boston: justin charles & co., 2003.

p079 shakespeare, william. "sonnet 18." *shakespeare: the complete works.* ed. g.b. harrison. fort worth, tx: harcourt brace college publishers, 1968.

p080 wharton quote: wharton, edith. *a backward glace: an autobiography.* new york: touchstone, 1998.

p095 thompson quote: *funny face.* dir. stanley donen. perf. kay thompson. paramount pictures, 1957. film.

p099 paley quote: "personalities: babe paley." *voguepedia.* condé nast digital, n.d. web. 29 march 2012.

klee quote: klee, paul. *the diaries of paul klee, 1898–1918.* ed. felix klee. berkeley, ca: university of california press, 1964.

p121 apfel interview: chase, edna woolman, and ilka chase. *always in vogue.* garden city, ny: doubleday & company, inc., 1954.

p129 auden quote: auden, w. h. "death's echo." *collected poems.* ed. edward mendelson. new york: random house, 2007.

p140 bergman quote: singer, irving. *ingmar bergman, cinematic philosopher: reflections on his creativity.* cambridge, ma: mit press, 2007.

p149 baumwell quote: white, alex w. *thinking in type: the practical philosophy of typography.* new york: allworth press, 2005.

p176 miller quote: miller, henry. *big sur and the oranges of hieronymus bosch.* new york: new directions publishing corporation, 1957.

p179 earheart quote: "quotes by amelia earhart." *amelia earhart: the official website.* family of amelia earhart, n.d. web. 1 april 2012.

p180 lovecraft quote: schultz, david e. and s. t. joshi, eds. *an epicure in the terrible: a centennial anthology of essays in honor of h. p. lovecraft.* cranbury, nj: associated university presses, inc., 1991.

p188 brontë quote: brontë, emily. *wuthering heights.* eds. william m. sale, jr. and richard j. dunn. new york: w. w. norton & company, 1990.

p197 carpenter quote: carpenter, liz. *getting better all the time.* new york: simon and schuster, 1987.

p205 parker quote: fitzpatrick, kevin c. *a journey into dorothy parker's new york.* berkeley, ca: roaring forties press, 2005.

p206 twain quote: garcia, nina. *the one hundred: a guide to the pieces every stylish woman must own.* new york: harpercollins, 2008.

p212 rilke quote: rilke, rainer maria. *letters of rainer maria rilke, 1892–1910.* trans. by jane bannard greene and m. d. herter norton. new york: w. w. norton & company, inc., 1945.

p216 emerson quote: emerson, ralph waldo. "hamatreya." *emerson: poems.* new york: alfred a. knopf, 2004.

p225 borges quote: borges, jorge luis. *seven nights.* trans. by eliot weinberger. new york: new directions publishing corporation, 2009.

p229 smith quote: smith, betty. *a tree grows in brooklyn.* new york: harpercollins, 2006.

acknowledgments

this book would not have been possible without the contributions of so many people. special thanks go to yael eisele, whose keen eye and savoire faire helped guide this project through twist and turn; dana lucas, who spun twenty years of ephemera into pure gold with her infectious enthusiasm; and sarah warren, whose gift for storytelling and sublime way with words quite literally brought *things we love* to life. additional gratitude is due to jeanette abbink, whose colorful spirit and meticulous design shines in each layout and line of type.

deborah aaronson and rebecca kaplan at abrams deserve much credit for first broaching the idea of a kate spade new york book and for being the perfect partners throughout the process. glenda bailey generously provided the foreword, and iris apfel kindly contributed many quotable gems to this volume.

lindsay knack was an early cheerleader of *things we love*, and theresa canning zast made many clever and colorful contributions to this collection. throughout these twenty chapters, deborah lloyd's creative flair and joie de vivre are apparent on every page.

kevin kwan contributed greatly in gathering photo credits and permissions, and linda dolan offered invaluable assistance fact-checking and sourcing the many quotes, quips and captions. amy gray offered essential editorial assistance later in the process and emily c. m. anderson helped polish the design.

last, but not least, *things we love* owes a great debt of gratitude to the entire kate spade new york team—both past and present—whose work could have filled a dozen more volumes just as delightful and engaging as this. *thank you.*

live colorfully